SCHOLASTIC News

Nonfiction Readers

Saturn

by
Christine Taylor-Butler

SCHOLASTIC INC.

New York Toronto London Auckland Sydney
Mexico City New Delhi Hong Kong Buenos Aires

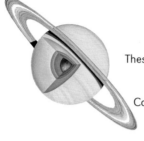

These content vocabulary word builders
are for grades 1-2.

Consultants: Daniel D. Kelson, Ph.D.
Carnegie Observatories
Pasadena, CA
and
Andrew Fraknoi
Astronomy Department, Foothill College

Photo Credits:

Photographs © 2005: Corbis Images/Jim Zuckerman: 5 bottom right; Finley Holiday Film: back cover, 5 top right, 9; Getty Images/Antonio M. Rosario/The Image Bank: 4 bottom right, 13; NASA: cover, 1, 4 bottom left, 5 bottom left, 7, 11, 17, 19, 23 right; Photo Researchers, NY/Lynette Cook/SPL: 2, 4 top, 15; PhotoDisc/Getty Images via SODA: 23 left.
Diagram on pages 5, 20-21 by Greg Harris

Book Design: Simonsays Design!

ISBN 0-516-25302-6

12 11 10 9 8 7 6 5 4 3 2 1   5 6 7 8 9 10/0

Printed in the U.S.A.   08

First Scholastic paperback printing, October 2005

CONTENTS

WORD HUNT

Look for these words as you read. They will be in **bold**.

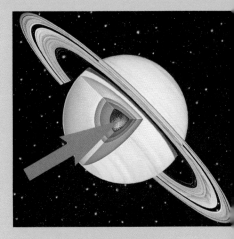

core
(kor)

Saturn
(**sat**-urn)

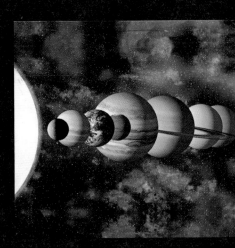

solar system
(**soh**-lur **siss**-tuhm

orbit
(**or**-bit)

ring
(ring)

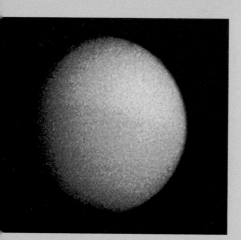

Titan
(**ti**-tuhn)

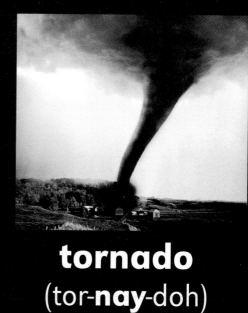

tornado
(tor-**nay**-doh)

5

Saturn!

Saturn has **rings**.

The rings **orbit** around the planet.

Saturn's rings are made of ice.

Can you skate on Saturn's rings? No.

The rings are not solid. There is ice but also dust, dirt, and empty space, too.

Other planets also have rings.

But Saturn has the most rings.

Scientists think there are 10,000 rings or more around Saturn.

Saturn's rings are very wide and very flat.

There are more than 30 moons that orbit around Saturn.

The largest moon is **Titan**.

It is the only moon that has air and clouds.

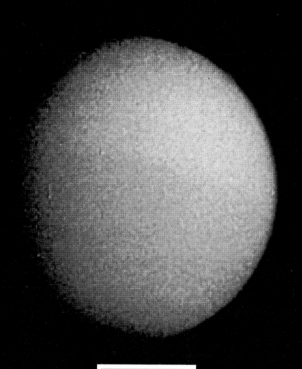

Titan

Saturn is the sixth planet from the Sun.

Saturn is the second largest planet in the **solar system**.

All the planets in the solar system orbit the Sun.

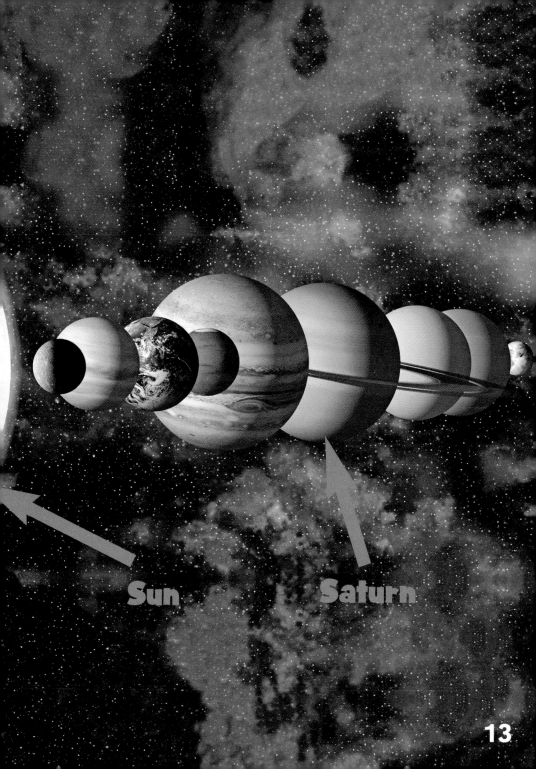

Sun

Saturn

Saturn is a giant ball of gas.

Deep inside the planet the gas becomes a hot liquid.

At the very middle of the planet is the **core**. The core is made of rock and ice.

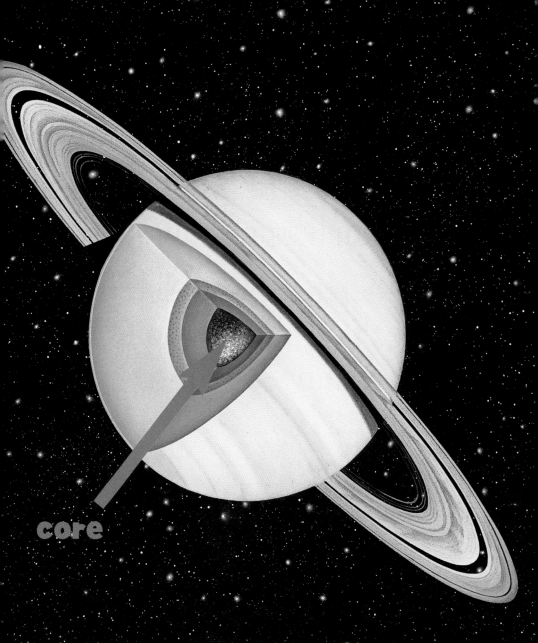

core

On Saturn, the wind blows very fast.

Sometimes the wind blows 1,100 miles per hour.

That is ten times faster than the winds inside a **tornado** on Earth!

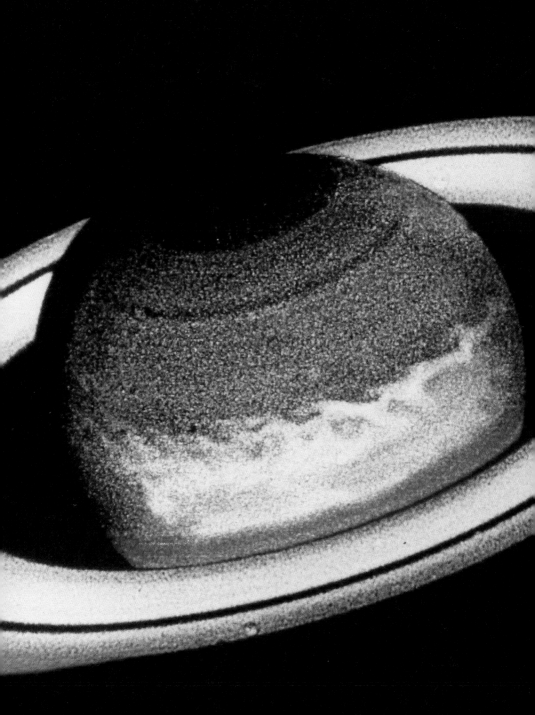

Saturn is very big,
but it is one of the
lightest planets.

One of the gases it
is made of is helium.

That's the gas that
makes balloons float!

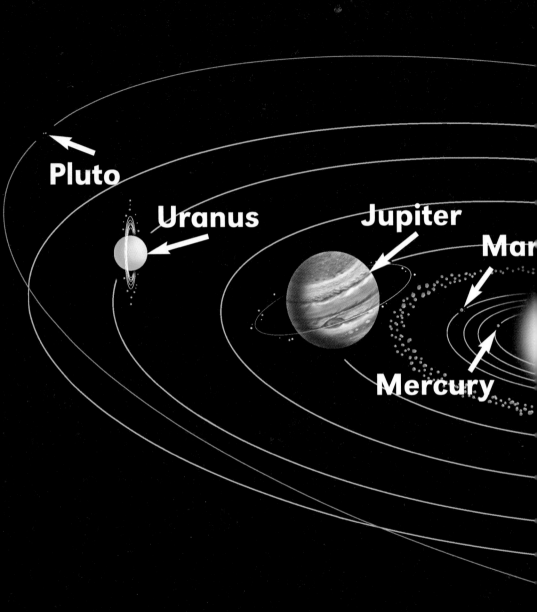

Pluto

Uranus

Jupiter

Mar

Mercury

SATURN

IN OUR SOLAR SYSTEM

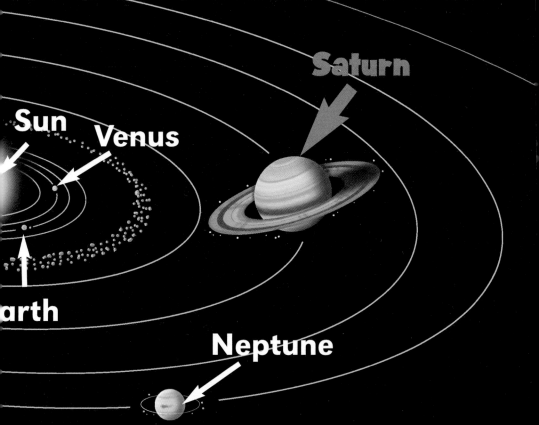

Saturn

Sun

Venus

Earth

Neptune

YOUR NEW WORDS

core (kor) the inside of a planet

orbit (**or**-bit) the path around an object

ring (ring) a band of rocks, dust, and ice that circles around a planet

Saturn (**sat**-urn) a planet named after the Roman god of the harvest

solar system (**soh**-lur **siss**-tuhm) the group of planets, moons, and other things that travel around the Sun

Titan (**ti**-tuhn) the largest moon of Saturn

tornado (tor-**nay**-doh) a funnel-shaped windstorm

Earth and Saturn

A year is how long it takes a planet to go around the Sun.

 Earth's year =365 days

 Saturn's year =10,756 Earth days

A day is how long it takes a planet or star to turn one time.

 Earth's day = 24 hours

 Saturn's day = 11 Earth hours

A moon is a big rock that circles a planet.

 Earth has 1 moon

 Saturn has 33 moons with more being found all the time

Did you know that you can fit 50 Earths inside of Saturn?

INDEX

FIND OUT MORE

Book:
Children's Atlas of the Universe
By Robert Burnham
Reader's Digest Children's Publishing, Inc., 2000

Website:
Solar System Exploration
http://sse.jpl.nasa.gov/planets

MEET THE AUTHOR:
Christine Taylor-Butler is the author of more than 20 books for children. She holds a degree in Engineering from M.I.T. She lives in Kansas City with her family, where they have a telescope for searching the skies.